D1810254

From the Depths
prayers from within bereavement

John Elliston

kevin mayhew

First published in 2005 by
KEVIN MAYHEW LTD
Buxhall, Stowmarket, Suffolk, IP14 3BW
E-mail: info@kevinmayhewltd.com
www.kevinmayhew.com

9 8 7 6 5 4 3 2 1 0
ISBN 1 84417 384 4
Catalogue No. 1500788

Cover design by Quetta Trueman
Edited and typeset by Marian Reid

Printed and bound in Great Britain

CONTENTS

ACKNOWLEDGEMENTS

I humbly acknowledge within these pages all those people whose grief I have been privileged to both share and to observe in the course of my work as a pastor. It is they, more than anything else, who convince me that death does not have the last word.

About the Author

The Reverend Dr John Elliston is a Baptist minister, currently working at Grange Road Baptist Church in Darlington. He has written a number of books of prayers including *Here in our Midst*, *Footprints on Sand*, *From the Foot of the Cross*, *Walking With Pain* and *Walking the Way of the Cross: Prayers For Your Personal Journey*.

PREFACE

The Church is adept at praying for the bereaved, but such prayers are, by definition, one step removed from the bereavement experience. The prayers contained in this collection are written from within grief, from the perspective of the one who has recently suffered loss. They represent the struggle to pray through, and to find God within, the greatest threat to our common humanity – the death of someone we love.

INTRODUCTION

Death is part of being human. In one sense, therefore, it is a very natural event. However, the fact that it can be rationalised does little to assuage our grief, particularly when the grief is new.

The following prayers are written from within the experience of bereavement. Although everyone responds differently and in a unique way to the death of someone close to them, the bereavement journey can be mapped against some of its characteristic stages. Not everyone will experience every stage upon which the prayers reflect (and the reader should feel no guilt where this is so for them). Also the timing and the intensity of the emotional response that a death elicits will vary. However, if within your own experience of grief, something that is present within these pages strikes a familiar chord, and if as a result you are helped to pray through and to offer to God the parting which death involves, the intention behind the writing will have been fulfilled.

1

THE FACT OF DEATH

The sunset is beautiful because it is a metaphor of ourselves. We are rainbows just before darkness, playing colours before night arrives. Even the lightest of Mozart's sonatas has the same drop of sadness, because sooner or later the final chord will be played. And there will be silence and nostalgia before the 'no longer'.*

Lord our God,
since my earliest years I have been surrounded by
    death;
through the anaesthetising glass of the television
    screen,
within the experience of neighbours and friends,
and sometimes, I have sensed it coming close.
But nothing prepared me for this day,
for the look, the touch, the smell,
of the death of someone I love.

Everything is silent,
everything is still;
there is a physical silence that I understand –

---

* Ruben A. Alves, *The Poet, The Warrior, The Prophet* (Edward Cadbury Lectures, 1990).

no breath,

no voice,

no movement –

but the silence is more than physical;
it has possessed me, invaded me, taken over my
   soul.
It is as if I, too, have died.

Lord, as I confront this awful silence,
and struggle to become reconciled
to the powerlessness of this moment,
the powerlessness of words
to say what still needs to be said,
the powerlessness of touch
to cajole lifeless limbs,
the powerlessness of will
to break down the impenetrable wall,

may I know that love is not bounded in this place,
that through the silence
and the inarticulate loneliness of this moment,
the voice of love is still heard,
and though the distance between life and death
   seems so very far,
in love may I sense that my beloved is just a step
   away.

Amen.

2

INCREDULITY

> I watched as the catafalque carrying my beloved descended, and my whole being was crying out: Come back!

Lord, still I cannot believe it.
Death is something that touches other lives, not
    mine.
He* was so full of life,
he was so vital and warm and hopeful.
How can this object of my love be no more?

I find myself reluctant to talk,
even to confide in a friend,
as if to talk about death
is to accept its reality
and seal the event in permanence.
But it is not permanent within me:
my ears are attuned to hear his voice,
my consciousness alert to respond
to his footsteps on the stairs,

---

* Throughout this collection of prayers the gender of the deceased alternates from male to female in successive prayers, allowing the reader the freedom to adapt the prayers to specific circumstances.

my mind waiting
for someone to tell me it is all a mistake,
a cruel but yet forgivable joke,
and so reverse the utterly irreversible.

Lord, the crisis, the mystery, the threat of death,
defy belief,
render me speechless,
throw me into confusion;
the sundering of love, of attachment, of relationship,
leaves me naked and exposed.
All I want is to undo this terrible pain,
to declare the game over
as in the *once upon a time* land of childhood play.
But there can be no pretending,
no fantasy of denial, no return to yesterday.
This death is real, and, however unpalatable,
I must accept this bitter cup
and drink its painful draught.

Gracious God,
as the reality of death breaks upon my consciousness,
and in the death of my beloved
I recognise our fragile finitude,
grant me to know your reality,
so that in coming to terms with what is close to me,
I may come to terms with what is beyond me,
and there discover that it is life, and not death,
that has the last word.

Amen.

3

NUMBNESS

Lord, I feel nothing;

my flesh no longer trembles,
the tears have dried up,
there is an emptiness within
that has spilled over into my heart,

and the aching centre of my being
is able to give no more.

Grief is somehow out there, not part of me,
its stark reality an illusion.
I am the spectator of its pain,
not a participant in its torment.
Detached, I try to make it real,
recalling the passing in every intimate detail,
the last look, the last touch, the last word,
trying to kick-start the mind to do justice to the
    love,
guilty at my apparent indifference, and questioning.

Perhaps I didn't really love her?
Perhaps my belief that she was everything
was but an illusion?
Perhaps it hasn't really happened at all!

Lord, when I am numb,
when my emotions are locked in cold paralysis,
when I erect walls
because my broken heart can take no more,
grant me, and those around me,
the wisdom to know
that this is but a halting place in my grief,
and not the final destination,
that what I fail to feel is a measure
of neither the intensity of my loss
nor the depth of my love,
that within all suffering
there is a natural (God-given?) anaesthesia.

Gracious God,
give me the courage to accept,
against all the evidence,
that I am neither unloving, nor unfeeling,
nor indifferent to the fact of death,
and in your good time,
free me to cry, to feel the loss and to hurt again.

Amen.

4

SHOCK

There is a time for everything, and a season for every activity under heaven . . . a time to weep and a time to laugh, a time to mourn and a time to dance.

Ecclesiastes 3:1,4

Lord, it is like being afraid,
being grasped by a stranger whose face I
  cannot see,

by a cold touch I do not recognise,
by an intention I do not comprehend.

Screaming, but no scream comes,
crying, but no tears,
running, but nowhere to hide.
Frozen in time, and place, and situation,
I struggle for an appropriate response.
Struggle to reconcile the inner conflict
between belief and unbelief.
Struggle to bring my reeling mind
into a semblance of rationality.

Holy Father,
grant me strength in these moments,

so that the awful truth I now confront
may not overwhelm or diminish me,
but may be faced and coped with in faith,
so that through faith
I may discover the means of interpreting this death
as a part of your love,
and through faith, I may find the resources
to live the tomorrows of this life
with the sure and certain knowledge
that the life of my beloved is within you.

Gracious Father,
help me to trust all that I know of you,
help me towards truth,
and may the knowledge of your perfect love
cast out all my fear.

Amen.

5

ANGER

In her poem 'Dirge Without Music', the poet Edna
St Vincent Millay (1892–1950) expresses succinctly
the anger which death can provoke:

> I am not resigned to the shutting away
>   of loving hearts in the hard ground.
> So it is, and so it will be, for so it has been,
>   time out of mind:
> into the darkness they go,
>   the wise and the lovely. Crowned
> with lilies and with laurel they go; but I am not resigned.

Why, God?
Why?
What is the meaning of this pain that robs,
that judges, that crucifies our humanity,
and which seems so arbitrary and so unheeding of
    gift,
or potential, or love?
Lord, he brought so much joy into the world;
Lord, he had so much still to give.
What is this wastefulness that is death,
that commits all that is not shared to oblivion,
and hides what might have been
in the darkness of eternity's impenetrable night?

You are the author of death,

to the beginning, you also gave an end,
to the opening, a conclusion,
to the act of creation, a cry 'It is finished!'

The responsibility is yours . . .

Lord, anger is part of my grief,
yet it is but the clothing of my fear;
fear that I too am mortal and will one day die,
fear that I will not cope alone,

fear that to be without him
is to lose everything that really matters.

Holy Father,
the anger that I now feel within me,
I have recognised in Christ –
you were silent before his anger and you are silent
     now:

'Eli, Eli, lama sabachthani?'

Grant me grace,
that I may know consolation,
not in receiving the answer to my 'Why?',
but in the fact that the hands which hold me
are nail-pierced,
and the love which embraces me
is understanding.

Amen.

6

LONELINESS

To be bereaved is to be alone. As Emily
Dickinson observes, parting is all we know of
heaven and all we need of hell...

Lord, she is gone, and I am alone;
no voice, no footstep, no loving touch,
no familiar face.

People try to comfort me,
to speak consoling words,
but they are not her words;
to extend a comforting embrace,
but it is not her embrace,
to share a sympathising tear,
but they are not her tears;
everything is bathed in futility.

On the corner of every street I search for her,
chasing the dark shadows of irrepressible yearning,
longing to see, to hear, to touch,
just once more the person that once was,
but all is emptiness and all is pain.

Gracious God,
the isolation I feel in loss is part of love,

for if I had not loved
I would not know the feelings
that now overwhelm me.
Grant me the courage
not to allow the loneliness I feel
to become self-pity,
nor longing bitter regret,
nor fear an instinctive rejection
of all who come near;
rather, lead me to discover the healing
that comes through other people,
those who are prepared to sit with me
and listen
as I tell the same story again and again,
those who remind me
that though I feel I have lost everything,
everything is not lost,
those who have stood where I now stand
and who have found a way through.

Gracious God,
when I am pleading to you for help,
grant me sufficient insight,
that I may see what you have already given
and be glad.

Amen.

7

GUILT

Guilt can often be present when someone dies. In grief we are extremely vulnerable, and when we are in such a condition what is negative often usurps a balanced view. Guilt frequently emerges when death causes us to reflect over-critically upon a relationship that we have lost.

Lord, when he was alive
I believed I had given him everything,
but now he is gone,
I feel the weight of lost opportunity
and a terrible sense of my own inadequacy;
the wasted minutes, and hours, and days,
when I was too slow to forgive,
the times when I let him down or caused him pain,
the angry (and unjust) words
with which I sometimes reduced him to tears;
all this comes flooding back into my mind,
the baggage of yesterday's guilt
adding to the weight of today's pain.

Lord, I feel guilty
that he cannot share the meal (his favourite)
that lies before me on the table;

I feel guilty that I am alive and he is dead
(I had selfishly hoped that I would die first);
I feel guilty when I laugh,
as if to crack the ashen face of mourning
with the sound of merriment
is a betrayal of the love that has bound us
through the passing years;
but most of all I feel guilty
that for a moment I forgot him –
a fleeting second when he did not fill my mind.

Gracious Father,
help me to live with the mistakes of yesterday
so that the memory of loving remains undistorted;
may I look upon the past with eyes that see truly,
on the one hand not denying
those things that were wrong,
but on the other not over-stating them,
for forgiveness is not invalidated by death,
and mercy is not hampered by the grave.

Help me also to recognise that in grief
I am judged neither by man nor God,
that mourning has no orthodoxy
by which my conduct is measured,
and that the guilt I now feel at the strangest things
is not the product of error, but of love,
struggling to find a new way.

Amen.

8

WHAT LOVE CAN DO

The days between a death and the funeral usually pass quickly. In part this is because the reality of the event has still to make itself felt, but in part it is because there remain practical things that love can do for the one who has died. The preparation of the funeral, the choices that still need to be made, the need to inform people of the passing, are all practical ways of loving the person who has died.

Lord, the smallest things seem so important . . .

the choice of a hymn,
the selection of flowers,
the memories that need to be publicly rehearsed.

My mind tells me they do not matter,
but my heart declares that they are everything –

for they are all that love can do . . .

All that I can do for her whose love has sustained me across the months and years,
all I can do for her for whom the stars represent no
   limit,

all that I can do for her whose flesh I have held
but whose cold body no longer responds
to the warmth of my embrace.

Lord, death steals but it does not triumph,
separates, but does not finally divide;
damages, but it does not ultimately destroy.

Holy Father, may the small things I can do
become the signs of a continuity that is greater
   than death,
– a declaration that love does not die,
a repudiation of death's claim to finality,
an affirmation that the essence of the relationship
that was still remains,
but that I must learn to live with my beloved in
   new ways.

Help me to recognise the profound significance
of what now seems trivial,
so that through it I may just glimpse
an Easter in the Holy Saturday of my bereavement.

Amen.

9

DEPRESSION

Depression is a natural reaction to loss. It is not an illness (though is sometimes treated as such). The death of someone close involves intense emotional concentration; depression in grief is a kind of emotional retrenchment, a period of convalescence for a battle-scarred mind.

> Pain has an element of blank;
> it cannot recollect
> when it began, or if there were
> a day when it was not.
>
> It has no future but itself,
> its infinite realms contain
> its past, enlightened to perceive
> new periods of pain.*

Lord, nothing matters any more.
The world is shrouded in a grey bleakness,
a joyless and drab monotony, a hopeless despair;
the struggle to go on living possesses a futility

---

* *Emily Dickinson*, ed. R. Wilbur (Dell, 1960), The Laurel Poetry Series, p. 75.

that makes the prospect of my own death
shine like a jewel,
life without him has no attraction.
Would that I could know
the anaesthetising black-out of the senses
which is eternal sleep.

Lord, in this symphony of grief,
even my body plays a part –

my limbs are heavy with exhaustion,
but no sleep comes,
my stomach can take no food,
my flesh is drawn to experience unknown ills
and to feel unrecognised pains.

Is death contagious?
Does it move from body to body like a plague?
Or is it simply as we have been taught,
that in the midst of life we are in death?

Gracious Father,
in the darkness of this experience,
grant me the tenacity to hold on more tightly
to what I believe than to what I feel,
to trust the instincts of my head
rather than the desires of my heart,
to listen to the certainties of yesterday
rather than to the doubts of today,
so that the truth by which I have ordered my life

may become my consolation,
and the discipline of faithfulness
become my reason to go on,
however mechanically.

Lord, until the daylight comes
and the veil of darkness falls away,
be close to me and hold me in love,
for I do not recognise these shadows
that embrace me from within,
I do not know myself and I am afraid.

Amen.

10

BECOMING RECONCILED TO DEATH

The most relevant thing at the time of death is the never-ending grace and mercy of God. Grief is the price we pay for love.

God our Father,
we are guests in the world, not permanent residents.
You have made us mortal and we must die;
the silver cord must be severed,
the golden bowl break,
the dust return to the ground it came from,
and the spirit return to the God who gave it.

Like the leaf that falls from a tree in the winter season,
so are our lives.

Gracious and loving God,
help me to accept the fact that someone I love has
    died,
not because all choice is denied to me,
but because painful as it is,
within death I can recognise, albeit partially,
the outworking of your purpose
and the operation of your grace.

For without death there would be no love,
without death no redemption,
without death no creativity nor an ultimate hope.

So Lord, in your mercy grant me courage,
that in my coming to terms
with the death of this person I love,
an element of thankfulness may be woven
into the pattern formed by tears –

thankfulness for the life
that has been and all that it has meant,
thankfulness for those things
that bodily death cannot sever,
thankfulness for the gift which death brings to love.

Holy Father, in the fullness of time,
when protest has left me and tears are spent,
may I discover,
as brother Francis discovered before me,
that behind the tragedy of death
there is a mystery with which life can be
    reconciled.

It is the mystery of the spirit's homecoming,
the mystery of mortality
becoming clothed in immortality,
the mystery of being gathered
into the Trinity of your love,
and being united eternally with you.

Thus may I recognise
that to become reconciled to death
is nothing other than becoming reconciled to you.

Amen.

11

LETTING GO

Lord, help me to live with the loss of today,
living as if through Holy Saturday,
so that tomorrow I may know the joy of Easter
  morning.

God our Father,
so much of our lives is letting go . . .

the innocence of childhood
lost to the exuberance of youth,
the burning passion of young adulthood
lost to the mellowing of middle age,
the visions and dreams of yesterday
surrendered to the real possibilities of today;

each a preparation, a rehearsal for pain,
but each so very far from the pain of this day.

Gracious God,
in the kingdom which in Christ you have revealed,

to let go is to hold,
to surrender is to take up,
to die is to live.

As I traverse the shock, the disbelief, the anger, the
 fear,
the yearning and the loneliness of grief,
help me as I learn to live with my beloved in new
 ways.
Lead me to recognise that my healing lies within grief
and not in avoiding it,
and teach me that hope is found in what I still have
 of her,
and not in what I have lost.

Lord, into your hands I surrender this body,
but the memories I hold are inviolate;
the walks in the park
and the moonlight playing by the edge of the sea;
the shared happiness and the shared sorrow,
the gentle reassurance of flesh touching flesh
as together we sought the gift of sleep.

Memories are both pain and joy,
holding and not holding
the promise of eternity and the final proof of
 mortality.

Lord, things will never be the same again,
but she whom I have loved and lost
is no longer where she was before,
she is now wherever I am.*

Amen.

---

* See John Chrysostom, over.

12

THE LOVE OF GOD

He whom we love and lose, is no longer
where he was before. He is now wherever we
are.*

Death must be placed within some meaningful,
ultimate context if life is to go on. It is given to the
angels to say: 'He is not here, he is risen.' But if we
talk of resurrection, we must never forget that there
is a place for tears.

God our Father,
you whose nature is love and whose way is holy,
in you all things exist and have their being;

nothing is beyond you,
nothing is outside your will,
nothing is irredeemable by your love.

Into your hands I commend the spirit of my
  beloved.

---

* John Chrysostom, fourth-century bishop of Constantinople

Gracious God,
in Christ you have shown us
that our bodies are but the seeds of mortality
that must be sown into the ground;

the harvest is immortality,
the harvest is freedom from pain,
the harvest is to live within the fullness of your
   holy, Trinitarian presence.

Grant me the grace to interpret this death within
   your love,
that as I surrender my beloved to you,
so in love you will receive *him*,
and insofar as I am also loved by you,
and insofar as *he* is loved by you,
so in love may we remain united?

Holy Father,
grant me the faith to believe
that love is stronger than death,
so that the love of this life touches the life to come,
and that the love of the life to come
sustains me now as I journey through pain.
May I have the courage to believe
those whom I have loved and who have died
are not forever lost,
so that they have merely gone before on a journey
that I too must make,

and that in your presence, and in your time,
there will be a day of blessed communion.

Lord, within the eternity of your love,
the communion of saints are no longer strangers,
they are the friends of my beloved.
Within you I love him, within you he loves me;
death has made no difference to our loving.

Amen.